This book is dedicated to the little artists around the world. May you color your world the way you imagine.

I am
Awesome!

I am Beautiful.

I am Confident.

I am Divine.

I am Empathetic.

I am
Generous.

I am
Helpful.

I am Joyful!

I am
Loved

I am

Nurturing.

I am Optimistic!

I am
protected.

I am a
Queen.

I am Responsible.

I am Victorious!

I am a Winner!

I give
XOXO
TO you.

I am
Zealous
for life,
as are you!

Aa

Bb

Cc

Create your own Affirmations!

1. _____

2. _____

3. _____

4. _____

5. _____

6. _____

7. _____

8. _____

9. _____

10. _____

11. _____

12. _____

13. _____

14. _____

15. _____

16. _____

17. _____

18. _____

19. _____

20. _____

21. _____

22. _____

23. _____

24. _____

25. _____

26. _____

Made in the USA
Middletown, DE
11 November 2021